In the Days of the
Dinosaurs

Roy Chapman Andrews

In the Days
of the
Dinosaurs

Illustrated by Jean Zallinger

Random House

New York

Contents

The Strangest Animals That Ever Lived   3

The World of the Dinosaurs   9

How Do We Know About Dinosaurs?   16

Bones Become Fossils   25

The Thunder Lizard   30

The King of Tyrants   35

The Duckbill   41

Dinosaurs With Armor   50

Dinosaur Eggs in Mongolia   58

What Became of the Dinosaurs?   72

Index   79

In the Days of the
Dinosaurs

The Strangest Animals
That Ever Lived

You have probably seen many animals besides pets.

The first one may have been a mouse. You have certainly seen rabbits and squirrels. If you live in the country, you may have met up with skunks, ground hogs, moles, opossums, badgers, chipmunks, raccoons, foxes, and deer. At the zoo you can

3

see strange animals from faraway lands: lions, tigers, monkeys, elephants, zebras, and giraffes.

But none are as strange as dinosaurs. They were the strangest animals that ever lived.

The word dinosaur (DIE no sawr) means "terrible lizard." Dinosaurs belonged to the family known as reptiles. Today snakes, lizards, and crocodiles belong to that same family.

A dinosaur's blood was cold, except when his body was warmed by the sun. Baby dinosaurs were hatched from eggs.

Millions of years ago, dinosaurs roamed everywhere on earth. They had many shapes

Baby dinosaurs

Reptiles of today—snake, lizard, and crocodile

and sizes. Some were no bigger than rabbits. Others walked on their hind legs and stood as tall as palm trees. They had short arms with long, curved claws.

Some dinosaurs were very, very big. One kind weighed more than ten elephants. It had a long neck and a small head. Its tail was as long as a school bus. This giant animal waded along the edges of lakes and rivers, eating the soft plants in the water.

One kind of dinosaur had short legs. It looked something like an army tank. Two long horns stuck out from its head like machine guns. Over its neck was a bony shield.

One of the most frightening dinosaurs

Reptiles of long ago—the dinosaurs

had a row of pointed plates down the middle of its back. Its tail was as long as a car, ending with four heavy spikes. Any animal that got hit by that tail would take off fast—if it could still move.

Another dinosaur had a heavy shell, like a turtle. At the tip of his tail was a great lump of bone. He could swing his tail like a war club.

Some dinosaurs were slender and swift.

They could run faster than a race horse. The very smallest dinosaurs hid among the rocks or in thick forests so they wouldn't be eaten by the big dinosaurs.

The World
of the Dinosaurs

Dinosaurs lived many, many millions of years ago. That was before there were any people. There were no warm-blooded animals like mice, rabbits, and lions.

No human being ever saw a dinosaur. All of these great lizards disappeared millions of years before men, women, and children appeared on earth.

9

The earth was a very different place in the age of the dinosaurs. There were no great mountains. But there were many volcanoes. The volcanoes shot fire and smoke and ashes into the sky and poured melted rock onto the plains.

The weather was much warmer then, and it stayed warm all the year round. Thick jungles and swamps stretched across most of the world. The warm weather was just right for dinosaurs and other reptiles.

Volcanoes in the days
of the dinosaurs

These cold-blooded animals needed warm
sunshine.

In those days the oceans were bigger
than they are today. Much of the United
States was covered by water. Kansas, Wyoming, Montana, Nebraska, Colorado, and

Dinosaurs in a swamp

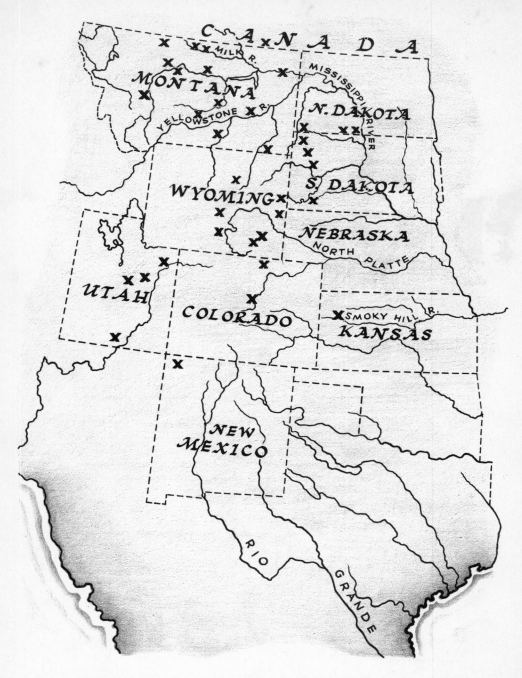

Dinosaur remains have been found at the places marked X
on this map—and in many other parts of the world

other states were at the bottom of this sea. Later the land rose and the water ran off.

In some places, there was dry land where we now have water. Today North America and Asia are separated in the north by a narrow strip of water. But in those days the two continents were joined by a strip of dry land.

Flying reptiles in the days of the dinosaurs

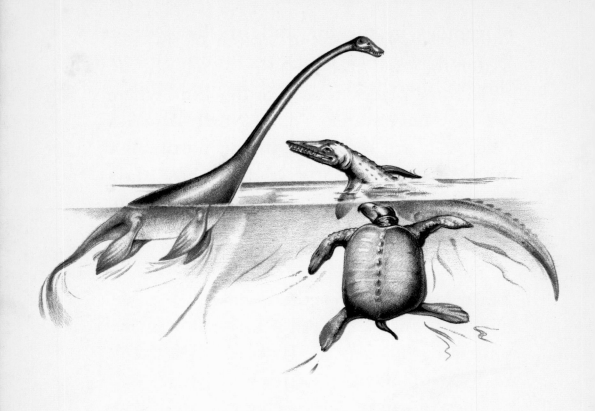

Strange sea creatures of long ago

The first animals could walk from one continent to the other. That is why dinosaur bones are found in many parts of the world.

The dinosaurs were not the only creatures in the world. There were other kinds of reptiles in the air and in the oceans. Not a single bird could be found. But in the sky there were strange flying reptiles. Some had wings that would have stretched across a city street.

Millions of years ago, the oceans had plenty of sea serpents. These creatures had wide, flat bodies. They had long necks and small heads filled with sharp teeth.

There were lizards in the oceans, too— lizards as long as telephone poles.

These animals would look to us like something from a bad dream. Did they really exist? Were they real?

They certainly were. The world was theirs for more than 140 million years.

How Do We Know

About Dinosaurs?

All of the dinosaurs died millions of years ago. *No man was alive to see them.* Then how do we know so much about them? How do we know what they looked like?

We know about dinosaurs from their bones. We have found many dinosaur bones. We have even found their eggs and their footprints. Does this seem hard to believe? Perhaps. The scientists themselves were puzzled when the first bones were discovered.

But over the years the scientists figured out the story of the dinosaurs. They worked very slowly. Sometimes they spent years putting together the bones from just one dinosaur.

The story began in 1818. The United States was a very young country then. Not a single railroad had been built. People

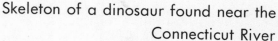

Skeleton of a dinosaur found near the
Connecticut River

traveled by wagon, by boat, on horseback, or on their own feet.

In 1818 some strange bones were dug up in the valley of the Connecticut River. No one knew what kind of animal they had come from.

A few years later, some strange teeth were found in the rocks of Sussex, England. The lady who found them took them to her husband, Dr. Gideon Mantell. He was both a doctor and a scientist.

Dr. Mantell had never seen anything

Dr. Gideon Mantell

like these big teeth. He showed them to other scientists. They said the teeth had probably come from a rhinoceros. But who ever heard of a rhinoceros in England? The rhinoceros belonged in Africa and Asia.

Dr. Mantell took some tools to the place where the teeth had been found. He dug very carefully and found a number of strange bones.

He studied the bones for a long time. Finally he decided they had come from a large reptile. The teeth looked like those of a living lizard, the iguana. So Dr. Mantell named the strange creature Iguanodon (ig WAN o don).

Later another British scientist gave this mysterious reptile a general name. He called it a dinosaur, meaning "terrible lizard."

Even before the first dinosaur bones were dug up, strange footprints had been discovered in solid rock. Nobody suspected that animals had made them.

Iguanodon

The first footprints were reported in 1802. That was only three years after the death of George Washington. A Connecticut farmer named Pliny Moody was plowing his corn field. His plow struck a buried stone. He dug it out. It was marked with tracks like those of a large bird.

Other stones with tracks were found. Years later people learned that the tracks had not been left by birds. They had been made by dinosaurs that walked on their

Farmer finding stones with footprints

Dinosaur footprints

hind legs. These dinosaurs had three toes on each foot.

But how could the dinosaurs make tracks in hard stone? They couldn't. The tracks were made along the edge of a river or a shallow inlet of the sea. Sometimes the water would spread over the shore, turning the hard ground into mud. Then the water would fall back.

The dinosaurs walked through the mud. Then the sun dried it and baked it. The footprints were as plain as a dog's tracks in a fresh concrete sidewalk.

When the water rose again, the footprints were filled with fine sand. After a great many years, the mud turned into hard rock. The giant tracks were still there. The water brought in more sand and mud, burying the tracks.

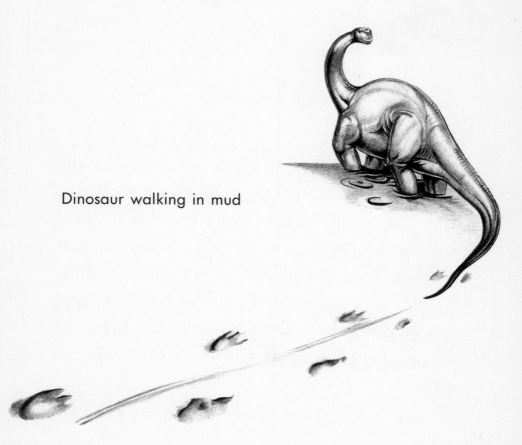

Dinosaur walking in mud

Footprint of a very large dinosaur

It was millions of years later that Pliny Moody plowed up the famous stone. There were the same tracks. They had been made by one of the thousands of dinosaurs that used to feed on plants in the river valley.

Dinosaur footprints have been found in many places besides Connecticut. Some of them are as long as the arm of a boy or girl.

Bones

Become Fossils

Scientists have learned much about dinosaurs by studying their bones. These bones have been buried for millions of years and have turned to stone. They are called fossils.

In Arizona, an entire forest was turned to stone. It is called the Petrified Forest. There you can see hundreds of fossil trees lying on the ground. Some are whole.

Others have broken into large chunks or small pieces. All of this wood was once buried. It became stone after thousands of years.

Some fossils show the print of leaves, ferns, and even insects. Long ago they lay in mud. After thousands of years the mud turned to stone.

These fossils tell us what the world was like millions of years ago. Fossils of palm trees and giant ferns have been found with

Fossil trees in the Petrified Forest

Fossil fern

the bones of dinosaurs. So we know they all lived at the same time.

Palm trees need warm weather. Giant ferns need plenty of rain. So there must have been more heat and rain than we have now.

At first, fossils were found only by accident. They might be found on hillsides where roads were being built. Or when a cellar was being dug. Or when a farmer plowed a field.

Usually fossils are not found on top of the ground. When scientists began to look

Palm trees and ferns in the days of the
dinosaurs

for fossils, they hunted in deep valleys and
canyons. They looked for places where the
rocks had been washed bare by rain and
running water.

The best place to look for fossils is desert
country. The ground is not protected by
trees and grass. Underneath there may be
bones that have been buried for millions of
years.

28

The desert gets much wind and some rain. In some places, the soil is blown away by the wind and carried away by the water. Then the bones underneath can be seen.

The Thunder Lizard

Perhaps you have seen a picture of a dinosaur in comic books. Probably it was the great Brontosaurus (BRON toe SAWR us). The "Bronto" part of his name comes from the Greek word for thunder.

A scientist named this animal. When it walked on the earth, he said, it must have made a sound like thunder.

Comic books often show Brontosaurus chasing people through the jungle. Of course this never happened. The dinosaur lived 100 million years ago, and no men were alive then.

The Brontosaurus, or Thunder Lizard, was 60 to 70 feet long. It would take two schoolrooms, without any ceilings, to hold him. He weighed about 80,000 pounds. This is more than ten elephants.

Brontosaurus had a long tail, and a long neck with a very small head. His brain was only half as big as yours. Yet his body was about 800 times as big. No wonder he was stupid. He was about as stupid as an animal could be and still live.

His mouth was very small. The teeth were so weak that the Thunder Lizard had to eat all day long. He spent his life wading in swamps and in the shallow water of lakes and rivers. With his long neck he could easily reach the plants he liked.

The water helped support his huge body. His legs were as thick as tree trunks.

Brontosaurus (Thunder Lizard)

Because Brontosaurus was so heavy and awkward, he was not a fighter. To protect himself, he stayed close to the water. When he saw one of his dinosaur enemies coming after him, he pushed out into deep water. The other dinosaur could not follow him there because it could not swim.

The American Museum of Natural History in New York has the skeleton of a great Thunder Lizard. His bones were discovered in Wyoming in 1898. Three men

Finding the bones of
Brontosaurus

worked six months to take out the skeleton, piece by piece.

Men at the museum spent four years putting together the broken parts. Some bones were missing. The museum experts made plaster bones to take their place. By studying the real bones, they knew what the missing ones looked like. Now the whole skeleton stands just the way the dinosaur stood long, long ago. It is 67 feet long and 15 feet high.

Skeleton of Brontosaurus

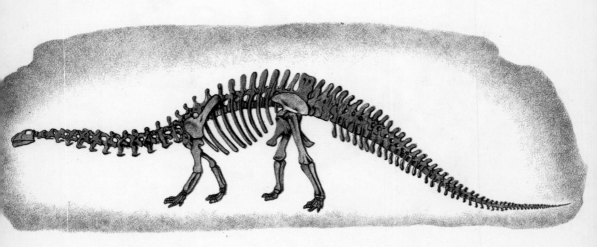

The King

of Tyrants

Imagine the shore of a lake near what was then the great inland sea of Montana. It is millions of years ago. There are many fig trees, palms, and banana trees. The day is hot. Mist hangs over the water.

A large dinosaur, called a Duckbill, moves slowly along the shore. He pushes his broad bill into the mud. He finds soft

bulbs and trailing water plants—food he loves.

Suddenly the Duckbill hears a sound. He sees a huge figure. It is a Tyrannosaurus (tie RAN oh SAWR us). This great dinosaur stands among the trees at the edge of the forest. The ugly head reaches up to the high branches.

Wild with fear, the Duckbill dinosaur hurries toward the water. But he can't move his fat body fast enough. The great Tyrannosaurus makes two jumps. He lands on the Duckbill's back. Six-inch teeth clamp shut on the Duckbill's neck. In a few moments, the struggle is over. As usual, the victor is the King of Tyrants, Tyrannosaurus Rex.

Tyrannosaurus rises on his hind legs and looks about. His body is as long as a freight car. His head is huge. His jaws are almost 4 feet long. His front legs are short and

Tyrannosaurus Rex
(King of Tyrants)

Battle of two dinosaurs

small. But they end in claws that are like iron. Tyrannosaurus is the most terrible animal that ever walked on earth.

With his teeth and claws, the killer tears the flesh from the Duckbill. He gulps it in huge chunks. At the end of an hour, half the skeleton lies bare. The killer's stomach is full.

Slowly the great dinosaur walks to the

Hills of Montana where
scientists found bones of the
King of Tyrants

King of Tyrants sleeping

jungle. There he stretches out beneath a palm tree. For several days he sleeps soundly. No other dinosaur dares to bother him.

Then Tyrannosaurus wakes up, hungry again. He goes forth to make another kill. That is his life—killing, eating, and sleeping.

The Duckbill

The Duckbill dinosaur had a mouth shaped like a duck's. But this dinosaur had 2,000 teeth. They were arranged in rows, one on top of the other. As soon as one tooth wore out, another pushed up from underneath to take its place.

The scientific name of the Duckbill is Trachodon (TRACK oh don).

The Duckbill was about 30 feet long. He was as tall as a one-story house. So he was not a little fellow by any means. Still, he was not more than half the size of the King of Tyrants.

He was something like a kangaroo. He had short arms, long hind legs, and a wide thick tail. Most of the time he walked on his hind feet.

The fingers of his small hands were joined by skin. Each hand was like a duck's foot. Trachodon used his hands as paddles in the water. His heavy tail also helped to make him a good swimmer.

This dinosaur loved the water. Here he was safe from the King of Tyrants and other killers who could not swim.

More skeletons of Trachodon have been found than of any other large dinosaur. There must have been a great many Duck-bills. They lived mainly on water plants.

Trachodon (Duckbill)

Probably they ate a few helpings of fresh-water clams from time to time.

One of the most exciting fossils ever discovered was the mummy of a Duckbill. It showed exactly what the skin was like. Usually a scientist finds only the bones. Often they are broken, and many parts are missing.

But in 1908 a scientist uncovered a Duckbill mummy in Wyoming. It had been buried in sandstone.

This dinosaur had died naturally. There were no wounds. Probably the body had stayed in the sun for a long time. The sun had dried up the body, just the way it dries up grapes and turns them into raisins.

Then the water rose. The whole body was covered with sand and fine clay. After many years, the sand and clay became stone. The stone was molded in the shape of the dinosaur.

Finally the flesh and skin rotted and disappeared. But the stone mold showed exactly what the skin was like.

Duckbills feeding

Fossil of a Duckbill's skin

This mummy showed that the skin of the Duckbill was rough—something like the covering of a golf ball. The skin was quite thin.

A close relative of this dinosaur was Corythosaurus (kor ITH oh SAWR us). It had a high, bony ridge on the top of its head. This dinosaur was a good swimmer.

The first dinosaur ever described in the United States was Hadrosaurus (HAD ro SAWR us). He was a relative of the Duckbill. His bones were not lying in a canyon of Wyoming or Colorado. They were just a few miles from the city of Philadelphia. Workmen found them while digging in a pit at Haddonfield, New Jersey.

The mysterious bones were taken home

Corythosaurus

by the workers. Soon they were put on people's shelves around the neighborhood. Some people used them for doorstops.

Some years later, a Philadelphia man heard about the Haddonfield bones. He went to the old pit and dug out more of the skeleton.

Then he went from house to house, col-

A dinosaur bone used
for a doorstop

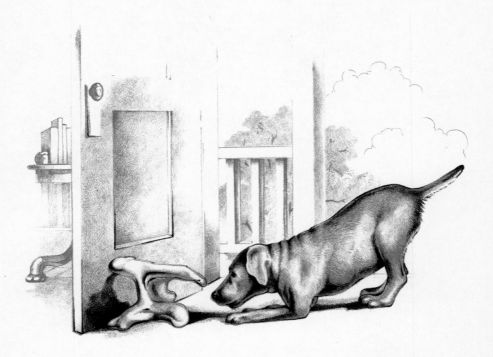

lecting the rest of the pieces. Finally he got enough to make a skeleton about as long as a schoolroom. The skeleton was named Hadrosaurus.

Dinosaurs

With Armor

If a dinosaur could swim, it could escape from its worst enemies. All it had to do was get into deep water very fast. The enemy was then left on shore, hungry and mad.

What about the dinosaurs that lived on land all the time? For thousands of years the smaller dinosaurs were eaten by the bigger ones. They were eaten for breakfast, lunch, or dinner—whenever they were caught.

Then, slowly, some of these dinosaurs developed a defense against being eaten. They began to grow bony plates like armor.

Over a long period of time, these plates got very thick. Even the King of Tyrants couldn't chew them up.

One of the armored dinosaurs was Stegosaurus (STEG oh SAWR us). He was about 15 feet long. He was built close to the ground, but was humped up behind. Down his back ran a row of pointed, bony plates that stood straight up. They were thin and sharp.

Stegosaurus had a powerful tail. At the tip were four huge spikes. Each was about three feet long. The dinosaur would swing this weapon from side to side. It could rip open the belly of an enemy much bigger than he was.

Stegosaurus was quite stupid. His body was bigger than an elephant, but his little

Stegosaurus

head had a brain no larger than a walnut. If he hadn't had such good armor, he wouldn't have lasted long.

Another dangerous tail was carried by Ankylosaurus (an KILE oh SAWR us). Like Stegosaurus, he had a low thick body. It was covered all over with bone plates. The tail ended in a huge mass of bone, like a club. It could crack the ribs of the largest dinosaur.

This fellow would plod along through the jungle. He wasn't afraid to meet Tyran-

Ankylosaurus

nosaurus. Even that monster could not bite through the bony plates.

One kind of dinosaur looked something like an army tank. He was almost as dangerous. This was Triceratops (try SER a tops), a word that means "three-horned face." His face was the kind you wouldn't want to meet except in a museum.

Two long horns stuck out from his enormous head. On his nose was the third horn, shorter than the others. At the back of his head was a great bony shield. His eyes were also protected by shields.

Triceratops was about as long as a telephone pole. His great skull was almost 10 feet long. All he ate was vegetables. He lived on land, but he wasn't afraid of the meat-eating dinosaurs. Probably none of those killers would risk being ripped open by the terrible horns of Triceratops.

Another horned dinosaur was called

Triceratops

Monoclonius (MON oh KLON e us). He had one large horn on his nose.

These tank-like animals and their relatives were the last of the dinosaurs. They came into the world late in the Age of Reptiles.

Monoclonius

Dinosaur Eggs

in Mongolia

In 1922, I organized an exploring party to hunt for fossils in Asia. We decided to go to the great plateau of Mongolia because it contains a desert. This is the Gobi, the greatest desert in Asia. We knew that bare land is the best place to look for fossils. The Gobi would be ideal, we thought.

Not many explorers had ever been in

Map showing the Gobi desert

the Gobi. It was not a friendly place. For miles upon miles, there was nothing but gravel with sagebrush, wiry grass, and thorny bushes. You could travel for days without finding water.

Only a few animals could live with so little water: gazelles, wild asses, and wolves. The gazelles and wild asses ate sagebrush until the wolves ate them.

The only people who lived in the Gobi were Mongols. Some of them had never seen a white man.

The desert was burning hot in summer. It was bitterly cold in winter when storms swept across it.

I was sure we could travel in the desert if we went by automobile. Cars would get us there quickly in the summer. And they

A native of the Gobi
desert

One of the Andrews automobiles,
with a cavalry escort

would get us out before the winter snow
came.

Others said this was a crazy idea.

"There are no roads," they said. "Only
camels can travel in that wild country. Besides, there is no reason to think the Gobi
will have any important fossils."

But we decided to go anyway. Some of

Camel of the Gobi desert

the world's leading scientists signed up for the trip.

We started from a little town near the Great Wall of China. We had forty men and eight cars. Our gasoline and supplies were carried by 150 camels.

The trail up to the Gobi desert was very bad. Deep ruts had been cut by the wheels of Chinese carts. There were mud holes and big rocks. Every few miles we had to stop and cool the steaming engines of our cars.

At last our cars got up the final steep slope. We passed through a narrow gateway in the Great Wall. Before us lay Mongolia. It was a land of deserts, grassy plains, and snow-capped mountains.

After two days we came to the edge of the Gobi. Here the ground was level. What we wanted was a place where the plain

Tents of the Andrews expedition

had been cut by rain into deep valleys. We wanted to see what was inside the ground.

The next day we found that kind of spot, and we put up our tents. Even before the tents were up, our men were looking for fossils.

And they found them. Those pieces of bone didn't look very important, but they were the first fossils ever found in that part

Finding the first fossils in that part
of the world

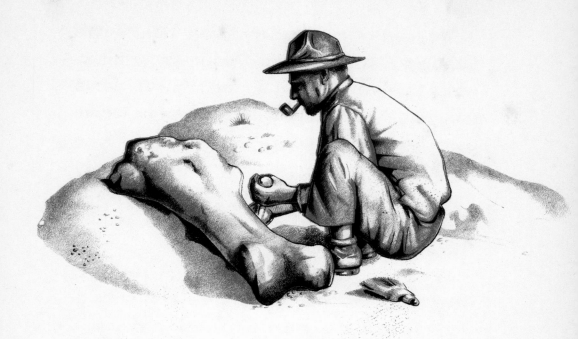

Dr. Walter Granger

of the world. We were so excited that we shook hands and laughed and shouted. We pounded each other on the back. Our expedition was a success.

These fossils were badly broken up. We couldn't be sure what kind of animal the bones had belonged to. But the next day one of the men called out: "Come with me. We have made a very important discovery."

We found one of the scientists, Dr. Walter Granger, on his knees. He was using a whisk broom to brush sand away from something in the ground. It was a great bone lying in the rock.

There was no doubt about it. This was the bone of a dinosaur. It was the first dinosaur ever known in Asia north of the Himalaya Mountains.

We made so many discoveries that we went back to the Gobi desert the next year. It was a wonderful hunting ground. But it wasn't a very safe place. A bandit named Kula and his gang were ready to attack or kill anyone they saw.

We carried rifles and revolvers in case we met up with Kula. Luckily we never did.

At one place in the desert, the setting sun made the red sandstone cliffs look as if they were on fire. We called this place the Flaming Cliffs. There were a great many

The Flaming Cliffs

fossils around the cliffs. So we put up our tents there.

Until then, no one was sure how baby dinosaurs were born. Scientists *thought* that they came from eggs. Dinosaurs were reptiles, and most reptiles lay eggs. But not one dinosaur egg had been found anywhere in the world.

On our second day at the Flaming Cliffs, George Olsen went for a walk. He came back with a strange story. He said he had found some fossil eggs. All of us joked about it. We were sure his eggs were nothing but round stones.

"Laugh if you want to," said Olsen. "But they are eggs all right. Come with me."

We followed him a short way. He pointed to a flat place in the rocks. There were three eggs, eight inches long. Dr. Granger picked one up. It was solid sandstone inside and quite heavy. The shell was broken, but it was a regular eggshell.

Dr. Granger finally said, "Gentlemen,

there is no doubt about it. You are looking at the first dinosaur egg ever found."

The three eggs had broken away from a shelf of sandstone. We could see the ends of other eggs in the rock. So we dug up the whole block of sandstone and sent it to New York, to the American Museum of Natural History. Later the rock was chipped away. Inside were thirteen beautiful eggs.

Pieces of white bone could be seen through the broken shells of two eggs. These bones were the skeletons of baby di-

Fossils of dinosaur eggs

nosaurs that had never come out of the eggs. They were named Protoceratops (pro toe SER a tops).

Two years later, we went back to the Flaming Cliffs. The wind, the frost, and the heat had been at work since our last visit. Sand had been blown away. Frost and heat had split the rocks.

This time we found dozens of eggs and many, many pieces of shell. This was a place where thousands of dinosaurs had laid their eggs.

But why hadn't these eggs hatched? It must have been this way: The mother dinosaur scooped out a shallow hole and laid her eggs. Then she covered them with a thin layer of sand.

She didn't sit on them, like a chicken, to keep them warm. The sun kept the eggs warm.

The little chick in a hen's egg gets air and warmth through air holes in the shell. Baby dinosaurs, still in the shell, also needed air and warmth. So the sand had to be thin and loose on top of the eggs.

Protoceratops

During a windstorm, many feet of sand were blown over some of the dinosaur nests. The deep sand cut off warmth and air. The eggs could not hatch.

Finally the heavy sand cracked the shells and the insides ran out. Then sand sifted into the cracks and kept the eggs from being flattened.

After many thousands of years, the sand over the eggs was pressed into rock. The sand inside the eggs turned into rock, too.

What Became

of the Dinosaurs?

Nobody knows why all the dinosaurs have disappeared. We can only make a few guesses.

Probably there were many reasons. The most important was that the world changed greatly. It was a very slow change. Instead of warm weather the year around, the winters turned cold. Many of the swamps and seas became dry land.

This was hard on the vegetable-feeding

dinosaurs that used to splash around in the lakes and swamps. They couldn't get enough to eat.

The birds and some animals today travel long distances to escape cold weather and get more food. But the dinosaurs were too big and too clumsy for long trips. They died of hunger.

This cut off the food supply of the King of Tyrants and all other meat-eating dinosaurs. These big fellows needed tons of meat. Even a fat Duckbill would last only a meal or two. When there were no more Duckbills, the meat-eaters died of hunger, too. They couldn't change their habits to keep up with the changing world.

If a man can't get meat, he can keep alive by switching to vegetables. Dinosaurs could not do that.

Perhaps another reason was that dinosaurs had very small brains. The giant Stegosaurus had a brain that was the same size as a kitten's. He didn't know how to keep alive when the world changed.

When warm-blooded animals appeared

on earth, the dinosaurs probably had new troubles. Some of these animals were furry little creatures, no bigger than a rat. They may have eaten the dinosaur eggs.

These warm-blooded animals became larger over millions of years. Their brains were much better than those of the dinosaurs. The cold-blooded dinosaurs were just too stupid. They couldn't hold onto the world that was once their own.

Dinosaur skeleton in a museum

Now only their bones are left. But from these bones we have learned an exciting story. We know what the world's strangest animals looked like. And we know how they lived, millions of years ago.

Brontosaurus
BRON toe SAWR us
(Thunder Lizard)

Ankylosaurus
an KILE oh SAWR us

Iguanodon
ig WAN o don

Corythosaurus
kor ITH oh SAWR us

Stegosaurus
STEG oh SAWR us

Trachodon
  TRACK oh don
  (Duckbill)

Triceratops
  tri SER a tops

Tyrannosaurus
  tie RAN oh SAWR us

Monoclonius
  mon oh KLON e us

Protoceratops
  pro toe SER a tops

Index

American Museum of Natural
    History, 33, 69
Ankylosaurus, 53
Arizona, 25
Asia, 13, 58, 66

Baby dinosaurs, 6, 68–70
Bones of dinosaurs, 19, 25, 27, 33,
    66
Brains of dinosaurs, 53, 73
Brontosaurus, 30–34

Colorado, 11
Connecticut River, 18
Corythosaurus, 46

Duckbill, 35–46, 73

England, 18–19
Eggs of dinosaurs, 68–71

Flaming Cliffs, 66, 68
Footprints of dinosaurs, 19–24
Fossils, 25–28, 44–46, 64–65

Gobi desert, 58–71
Granger, Walter, 66, 68
Great Wall of China, 62–63

Hadrosaurus, 46–49

Iguanodon, 19

Kansas, 11
King of Tyrants, 37, 40, 73

Mantell, Gideon, 18–19
Mongolia, 58, 63
Mongols, 60
Monoclonius, 57
Montana, 11, 35, 39
Moody, Pliny, 21, 24

Nebraska, 11
North America, 13

Olsen, George, 68

Petrified Forest, 25
Protoceratops, 70

Reptiles, 4, 10, 19, 68

Skeletons of dinosaurs, 34, 43, 69
Skin of dinosaurs, 44–46

Stegosaurus, 51, 73
Swamps, 10, 72

Thunder Lizard, 31–34
Trachodon, 41–46
Triceratops, 54
Tyrannosaurus, 37–40

Volcanoes, 10

Wyoming, 11, 33, 44

About the author of this book

Dr. Roy Chapman Andrews, scientist and explorer, was born in Wisconsin. His scientific expeditions have taken him into some of the most remote parts of the world—the Dutch East Indies, southwest China and Burma, northern Alaska, North China and Outer Mongolia.

For many years Dr. Andrews was Director of the American Museum of Natural History in New York. Now he lives in Carmel Valley, California.

His books for boys and girls include *All About Dinosaurs*, *All About Whales*, and *All About Strange Beasts of the Past*.

About the illustrator of this book

Jean Zallinger doesn't mind the fact that her three children keep an assortment of pets around the house. The household includes two boxer dogs, one iguana, two horned lizards, one leopard lizard, two parakeets, one snapping turtle, and numerous guppies. Mrs. Zallinger and her family live near New Haven, Connecticut.

She received a bachelor's degree from the Yale School of Fine Arts. Her scientific drawings have appeared in *Life, Natural History,* and other magazines. In 1958 she illustrated a book for boys and girls, *All About Monkeys.*